SUCCEEDING A
A ROADMAP TO OVEI
ACHIEVING SUCCESS

BY JAMIE SCHWANDT, Ed.D.

Cover photograph courtesy of Jami McDowell Photography

Published by Starry Night Publishing.Com

Rochester, New York

Jamie Schwandt, Ed.D.

Contents

Jamie Schwandt, Ed.D.

Dedication

This book is dedicated to Bob and Sharon Bearley, thoughtful foster parents who encouraged me to achieve rather than settle. Mrs. Bearley passed away in March of 2014; she was a warm and supportive foster parent who cared deeply for her family and foster children. The Bearley's have inspired many, both through their kindness and love. Those who have had the great pleasure of meeting Mr. Bearley are moved at his close relationship with God and his spirit of giving. Not only does Mr. Bearley personify the best qualities in mankind, he is the kindest individual I have ever met.

Jamie Schwandt, Ed.D.

Introduction

If you are reading this book, you are likely presently or formerly a foster child, or a current or prospective foster parent. As a former foster child myself, I know and can relate to what foster children experience as they navigate the foster system into adulthood. I understand the challenges foster children face daily, and I feel a deep obligation to help them work through their struggles while still celebrating their triumphs. This book is for foster children everywhere. Whether you choose to read this book from beginning to end or skim the chapters, my intention is that you take from it a powerful message about treading through the sometimes-murky waters of the foster care system.

My intentions for this book are not solely to discuss the plight of the underrepresented, but rather to assist former and current foster children and their foster parents to understand how to reach for and achieve success. This book will provide tools to overcome challenges as well as contribute to the knowledge foster children have about the great opportunities they have been afforded by simply being foster children. You read correctly; I used "opportunity" and "foster children" in the same sentence. Rather than be victims of circumstance, foster children have the power to achieve success using the power of thought. While indeed a challenging task, mastering this skill can and will change your life. This text will explain the importance of looking within and modifying your thinking as a mechanism for accomplishing goals. This book will discuss your road map to success in life and how to utilize the foster care system to your advantage. Finally, it will provide you with resources to utilize during and after foster care. This book will serve as a guide for you. Keep this book close to you and refer to it often. If you follow the steps outlined in this book, you will find success in life.

Jamie Schwandt, Ed.D.

Organization of Book

This book captures the advice of a former foster child while reporting the findings of Dr. Schwandt's significant research with foster children, including the perceptions of foster children who have exited the foster care system. The format of this book is that of a direct road map to success. Ten themes emerged from the research conducted by Dr. Schwandt. These themes (listed below) are referenced throughout the book and provide valuable direction for foster care children and the system. It is imperative that all parties involved with the development of foster children are aware and implement these themes for the success of these youth. The participants have provided a blue print to repeat to ensure current and future foster children have the support and resources necessary to be self-sustaining adults.

1. Participants were adamantly against re-integrating with their biological families.

2. School was an escape for foster children before they entered foster care.

3. Foster parents served as an important positive mentor in the young individual's life.

4. Foster children were confused and were not provided clear guidance when they were removed from their biological family.

5. The participants would not be where they are today if they would not have been placed in foster care.

6. The Kansas tuition waiver was instrumental to the participants' success.

7. Participants felt that they were not notified of the education benefits until it was nearly too late.

8. Participants were perceived to have a chip on their shoulder due to the negative stigma of being a foster child and used the chip as motivation.

9. Participants felt that being socially active was instrumental to their success.

10. Participants perceived that education was a key to attaining success in life.

Chapter Format

Foster Care Wisdom: An inspirational quote or message

Mile Marker: Provides guidance on what it takes to find success and discusses researched themes

Discussion: Provides insight from interviews conducted by the author and advice

Summary of Actions: Contains a detailed list on how to utilize each chapter in life

Take Away: Key message from that chapter

Foster Care Research

Little research exists highlighting the effectiveness and opportunities of the foster care system for current or former children. In 2013, the dissertation research conducted by the author, Exiting Foster Care: A Case Study of Former Foster Children Enrolled in Higher Education in Kansas, studied the strengths and emerging possibilities in foster care and the conditions that make them possible. Essentially, the study identified success stories of former foster children and determined how they did it. Fifteen former foster children who overcame significant obstacles and enrolled in post-secondary academic institutions in Kansas were interviewed. Success was defined as educational attainment since foster children severely lack in this area of achievement. The study yielded ten reoccurring themes from the interviews that can be used as a roadmap for achieving success for foster children. The study and quotes from interviews are used as the foundation for this book.

Jamie Schwandt, Ed.D.

Foster Care Statistics

Foster care is provided to children to prevent maltreatment and
abuse by providing a temporary or foster home. There are
approximately 400,000 children in foster care today. The foster care
system is structured to provide basic needs for a child and additional
resources for educational attainment or training, housing assistance,
counseling, and other services. The system is intended to create self-
sufficient adults. The objective is such that as children "age-out" of
foster care, they are able to obtain gainful employment, secure
housing, and nourishment on their path to becoming productive
members of society. The foster care system is an opportunity, if you
approach it as one. Unfortunately, this is not reality for many
children in the foster care system. According to 2009 research, the
following statistics demonstrate a poor outlook for foster children:

54% of foster children completed high school compared to 82%
of the general population (children not in foster care);

2% of foster children completed a bachelor degree compared to
24% of the general population;

25% of foster children had been homeless since exiting the
foster care system;

30% of foster children were receiving public assistance;

30% of foster children had no health insurance; and

51% were unemployed.

Statistics are grim, but the potential of each foster child is not.
These children have a unique opportunity to reverse these statistics
by bettering themselves. You are not defined by a percentage. What
defines you is your drive, your character, and your actions. Being a
foster child is an opportunity and a challenge. Embrace it!

Foster Care Stigma

As a foster child, you may be accustomed to feelings of shame and embarrassment. Perhaps you have felt demeaned or lesser than your peers. You may feel cast aside as you are repeatedly thrown into new homes—homes that are never quite yours. You feel uneasy, lack control, and again, this new space is not your own. The experience of becoming a foster child may be different for some, but for many it brings with it a negative stigma—a stigma of failure and emptiness. And while you had no control over the circumstances, you cannot help but feel inadequate. You feel as though your life is a string of failures with each impending negative thought infiltrating your subconscious. When people say you will fail and you are surrounded by nothing but failure, it's only natural that you start believing the message. It's time to change this mindset and eliminate this stigma.

Jamie Schwandt, Ed.D.

Chapter One: The Power of Positive Thought

Foster Care Wisdom:
"The mind is everything. What you think you become." –
Buddha

Mile Marker:
The power of positive thinking is vitally important. You may
have heard this before; however, it is without a doubt the purest form
of truth. Positive thought creates successful people. You can only
become what your mind tells you to become. Therefore, you must
train your subconscious to think positive, gratified thoughts while
eliminating negative thoughts. It is essential that you are aware of
your thoughts as well as how to control them. Take twenty seconds
and think about the last few thoughts you had. If your thoughts were
negative, replace them with something positive. For example, if you
thought, "I am bad at math," alter this negative consideration to
emphasize a subject that you do well in; such as, "I am really good at
biology," or "I like to learn new things."

Throughout the day, simply stop and ask yourself what you are
thinking and how you are feeling. Make this mindful reflection a
habit. In short, remind yourself to think about what you are thinking.
If you find yourself feeling down, thinking negative thoughts, or
simply having a bad day, stop what you are doing and fill your mind
with positive thoughts and words of encouragement. This skill
cannot be emphasized enough: you will become what you think
about most. If you feel like a failure and let disappointment control
your thoughts, you will become a failure. Controlling your thoughts
is a difficult task, but it can be accomplished overtime with regular
practice.

Moreover, by simply being a foster child, you may hold serious
doubts about the likelihood of succeeding. Unfortunately, these
feelings are typical and even expected. Why would you not have
these doubts? Judging from foster care statistics, it is not entirely
shocking to assume many people believe you will fail in life. When
only 2% of foster children will graduate from college, you may be
skeptical about your opportunity to attend college at all. This kind
of doubt is both toxic and counterproductive.

The key to eliminating these doubts and fears is by simply replacing the negative thoughts with positive ones. Once you become aware of the negative thoughts that are obstacles to your successful future, you have the power to change them. If you are considering attending college and doubt seeps into your thoughts, simply remove uncertainty and replace it with confidence or assurance that you too, are capable of reaching your objectives. Think about how exciting it will be to pick your class schedule, meet new people, and soak up all the new knowledge. Focus on how a college education can lead to greater financial independence or how it will feel to become the first college graduate in your family. Find the motivation to become part of the 2% of foster children who complete a college degree.

To employ positive thinking, each day find a quiet area—free from daily distractions—to clear your mind. Take some time to become aware of your thoughts and overall disposition. You are now going to do some "house-cleaning" in your mind. Remove all negative thoughts that enter your mind and replace them with something positive. Focus on ambitions, opportunities, talents, and accomplishments. This conscious effort will help to train the subconscious from focusing on failures while developing a positive attitude, despite obstacles and challenges that may arise. If you fully invest in these actions, you will notice a difference. Failure may still be around you, but you will no longer feel it defines who you are. Being a foster child will no longer carry a stigma of worthlessness; instead, you should feel empowered to seek and use resources to better yourself.

In addition to positive thinking, to be truly successful, you must clearly identify what you want in life. Determine what motivates you and outline the goals you want to achieve. This is not a time to think small—think big. Do not let your current situation inhibit you from developing your dreams and goals. Again, focusing on the negative aspects of life will only create a holding pattern; focus on positivity and plan for the future. Be determined despite your current situation. Your thoughts alone are the key element to your success. You must learn to formulate positive thoughts that will lead you to your desired goal. It is only natural to feel negative thoughts; thoughts of doubt, discord, discouragement, and failure plague many current and former foster children throughout the world.

Immediately replace these negative thoughts with thoughts of bliss, encouragement, joy, and positive expectation. Clear your mind of past failures, as this will only create the additional obstacle of dwelling on the past, eliciting failure in the future. Clear your mind of the fear of failing. Instead, envision yourself accepting your diploma on the commencement stage or walking into your first adult job with your head held high.

Constantly reminding yourself you will be a success story is the first step on a path unknown to many like you. Think about who you will become. Create a list describing the type of person you want to be. What characteristics are important to you? What will you strive for? How do you define success? Once you have jotted down a list, read it every day. For example, "I want to be strong, smart, faithful, a good friend, a good student, a healthy person, and a wealthy person." Repeat your list as you wake up in the morning and as you go to bed at night. Submitting these ideas to your subconscious will help you to visualize and become that person. However, you cannot simply just read aloud your list and expect change. You must follow through with action. If you want to be smart, then you must ensure you are taking appropriate steps that will bring this result. Education is key in attaining this goal. You must pay attention in class, formulate good study habits, begin thinking about college, and remain positive in this pursuit.

Furthermore, think of how great it will feel when you become a success. Take a moment and reflect on that last sentence. Picture the feeling of accomplishment and self-reliance. You can be part of the less than two percent of foster children who graduate from college. Perhaps you will go further; be a doctor, a lawyer, or a scientist. The possibilities are endless. Really think about that for a moment. You alone have the power to make your dreams reality.

Discussion:

"I just keep telling myself that I want to be able to provide for my kids. I want to be successful. That's what kept moving me forward, is that I don't want to be like my mother and father." Research Participant/Former Foster Child

As stated in the previous paragraph, you must follow up your positive thoughts with action. This action must be positive. Otherwise, what's the point? To do this, you must separate yourself from fear and doubt. If you speak with someone who discourages you from accomplishing your goal, then you must end the discussion and walk away. Do not discuss or read materials that will bring about negative thoughts and discourage you from who you want to be. Do not surround yourself with people who discourage you from becoming who you want to be. Surround yourself in a positive, flourishing environment. Do not associate with people who have no interest in furthering their own lives. For example, if you are with a group of people smoking marijuana or making other poor decisions, you are in the wrong environment. That should be an obvious statement. Do not discuss past failures and do not discuss your family or your circumstance negatively. Start discussing your life positively.

Focus on the present and the future. As a middle school or high school student, you will undoubtedly face some form of peer pressure or criticism. Practice blocking out negative influences and talk that prevents you from attaining your goals. If your goal is to become a teacher and you enter a discussion with someone who discourages you, simply thank him or her for the input and walk away. From a personal standpoint, I began writing this book in 2012, and after reaching out to different people, I got the impression my attempt would be a lost cause.

> "I just keep telling myself that I want to be able to provide for my kids. I want to be successful. That's what kept moving me forward, is that I don't want to be like my mother and father."
>
> Research Participant/Former Foster Child

Those comments stuck in my head, and after a long year, I realized I should have listened to my own advice. It is vital to surround yourself with positive people so that you can continue to reach for your goals.

Now that you understand how to control your thoughts, think positive and erase doubt, and surround yourself in a positive environment, focus intently on your goals in life. Envision your goal and think of nothing else. Focus on that goal every day. Start using your imagination and visualize achieving that goal. Form a clear picture of exactly what you want. Think about only what you want; once you have this clear picture in your mind, think about that picture every night before you go to sleep and again when you wake up in the morning. Visualize your goal regularly with every chance you get.

Summary of Actions:
1. Stop and think about what you are thinking and feeling; be aware of your thoughts.
2. Rid yourself of negative thoughts. Substitute negative thoughts with positive thoughts.
3. Immerse yourself in a positive environment surrounded by positive people.
4. Focus on your life goals. Create a list of your ambitions and decide to make them reality.

Take Away:
We all possess the same ability to either succeed or fail. Being a foster child and failure are not synonymous. Dream big, think positive, and take action. Your path to success begins with the power of positive thinking.

Chapter Two: Embrace the Opportunity

Foster Care Wisdom:
"A pessimist sees the difficulty in every opportunity; an optimist sees the opportunity in every difficulty." – Winston Churchill

Mile Marker:
For many, being a foster child is an opportunity for a better life and a life of possibilities that you may not had before. Being part of the foster care system is an opportunity. It's really no different than receiving a scholarship or being accepted into an organization that provides personal development. Granted, you did not ask for this nor did you apply for this. You may have also suffered severely before you entered foster care, but just think about this for a moment. You, most likely, left a bad situation where you painfully witnessed family members making the wrong choices. You may have even been abused or neglected. You have left that life and are now (hopefully) with a new family who will keep you from that lifestyle. You have an opportunity to start a new life with an abundance of resources and support that you MUST utilize—but more on this later.

Furthermore, whether you choose to believe it or not, being in a foster home is a good experience. There is a reason you were taken from your family; current research suggests that former foster children, who are currently in college, were adamantly against reintegrating with their biological families given the opportunity. These same participants have had ample time to reflect about their experiences.

The study revealed that the foster care system enabled foster children to be successful and that being removed from their families was instrumental in their journey to becoming a success story. On the contrary, one of the priorities for the foster care system is reintegration of children with their parents. Your time in the foster care system may be limited or may last into adulthood; regardless of the duration, use this time to determine the kind of life you want to lead.

Again, using positive thought from Chapter One and the resources and support through the foster care system, your current situation is truly an opportunity. You are no longer part of a destructive or neglectful situation which is good. This is a chance for you to thrive in a positive environment.

Discussion:

"A recommendation for something that needs to be changed in a lot of these states and agencies is their mission for kids put into foster care is reintegration. I feel like that is not necessarily the case for a lot of people. It shouldn't be reintegration; it should be the best interest of the child." Research Participant/Former Foster Child

Personally, I was reintegrated with my family, but I quickly realized this was a great error and was placed back into the system. I ended up staying away from my family and my life has flourished with success. I witnessed my younger brother, who remained with my family, follow a similar pattern of poor choices and self-destruction. He did not graduate high school, has been incarcerated, and struggles with drug and alcohol use.

My research findings indicate that foster care children are rarely able to be children while in custody of their biological families. Often providing care for siblings takes a toll on any child as was the case in my own life as my brother and I were left alone on multiple occasions. We had to fend for ourselves before we were placed in foster care.

"A recommendation for something that needs to be changed in a lot of these states and agencies is their mission for kids put into foster care is reintegration. I feel like that is not necessarily the case for a lot of people. It shouldn't be reintegration; it should be the best interest of the child."

Research Participant/Former Foster Child

"I was ten. Made supper, did dishes, did everything pretty much. And I also had my first job at ten. I had a paper route. We moved around a lot. I'd come home and my parents might be home or the other kids would be by themselves. So I'd take care of them, put them to bed, pretty much do everything by myself."

Research Participant/Former Foster Child

"I was ten. Made supper, did dishes, did everything pretty much. And I also had my first job at ten. I had a paper route. We moved around a lot. I'd come home and my parents might be home or the other kids would be by themselves. So I'd take care of them, put them to bed, pretty much do everything by myself." Research Participant/Former Foster Child

While sustaining emotional damage, some participants were physically and sexually assaulted. Many endured horrible conditions before placement in foster care. These findings indicate that reintegration is rarely in the best interest of the child. Foster care was an opportunity for these participants, many of which admitted they may even be dead if not for foster care. Each participant recognized the foster care system as the opportunity that brought success.

Being a foster child was a huge opportunity for me. I left behind a tumultuous life and lived with families who provided stable, nurturing environments. It was easy for me to recognize that the life I came from was not one I wanted to continue to live. While the foster care system may have flaws, in most situations, it eradicates children from a failing environment while giving the opportunity to thrive. Take advantage of your time in foster care. Use the resources and the caring individuals to build the life you want to have.

Summary of Actions:
1. Utilize this opportunity for your benefit. Find a quiet area to focus on the possibilities.
2. Briefly think about your past. Consider a life without the poor circumstances; you have just entered that new life.
3. Think about being a child. Focus on what you can do now with your new life.
4. Focus on your future goals in life. Do not think about the past anymore.

Take Away:
Help yourself and let others help you. Foster care is an opportunity. Embrace it!

Chapter Three: Seek out a Positive Mentor

Foster Care Wisdom:
"Tell me and I forget, teach me and I may remember, involve me and I learn." – Benjamin Franklin

Mile Marker:
Every person needs a positive mentor. This is a person you can turn to when you need advice and guidance. You must seek out your own personal mentors because they will not necessarily find you. You may find that you have multiple mentors in life. One individual may provide professional guidance, while another provides spiritual, and still another personal. As a foster child, it is vital to identify a mentor you can trust and learn from. Seeking a mentor may be as simple as discussing issues or having a conversation with a person you trust and look up to. Your foster parents may be excellent mentors to guide you through childhood into adulthood.

Finding a mentor is crucial as you navigate through the goals you have established and the new opportunities you embrace. The experiences you have with your new, positive outlook may be overwhelming. Your mentor can help guide you, answer questions, and connect you to additional resources. Strategically giving a person this role in your life is an important step in achieving your goals. A mentor is security, a person who can travel the journey with you.

"My foster parents are actually the ones that encouraged me to go to college."

Research Participant/Former Foster Child

Discussion:
"My foster parents are actually the ones that encouraged me to go to college." Research Participant/Former Foster Child

Foster parents can be excellent mentors. However, there are several people in your life who can fill this role. Seek guidance from your teachers, agency workers, priests, ministers, coaches, and trustworthy peers about your goals, concerns, and current situation. You have to ask questions. If a person continues to respond positively to your questions and you feel as though you can go back to them for support, then most likely they are turning into a mentor for you. Continue to seek their input and guidance as much as possible.

Moreover, research participants who had a foster parent serve as a positive mentor during their time in the foster care system are still in contact with these mentors today. For example, the participants celebrate birthdays, holidays, and graduations with their foster parents. Positive mentors will teach you additional skills such as leadership, conflict resolution, and resilience. In my experience, I have grown in my faith, learned to manage soldiers, and made big career decisions based on the actions I witnessed my mentors take. A good mentor is one who is also a proponent of positive thinking and one who fights to make the best of any situation. Good mentors will model good conduct you will mimic in your own life.

"I always felt that my foster parents were very hard working people. I bonded very well with them because they told me their life stories. Their work ethic, their sense of focus, and also their ability to reason through things to help me out and assessing my options so I can see where I'm going.

"I always felt that my foster parents were very hard working people. I bonded very well with them because they told me their life stories. Their work ethic, their sense of focus, and also their ability to reason through things to help me out and assessing my options so I can see where I'm going. If I gave them an idea of what I wanted to do, they supported it. They helped me look at tuition, and what criteria I needed to keep up. They helped me out with the letters of recommendation that I needed."

Research Participant/Former Foster Child

"If I gave them an idea of what I wanted to do, they supported it. They helped me look at tuition, and what criteria I needed to keep up. They helped me out with the letters of recommendation that I needed." Research Participant/Former Foster Child

Foster parents that serve as a positive mentor are vitally important to a child's success. They should provide you with advice, but it is your responsibility to ask questions to receive this advice. Ask simple questions such as how to set up a bank account, how to complete a job application, or how to obtain a driver's license.

These are life building skills that you must attain as a foster child. You must be ready to become a self-sufficient adult upon exiting the foster care system. A self-sufficient adult must understand how to get a job, manage a bank account, pay bills, purchase a car, apply for college, obtain health insurance, find a place to live, cook, and manage other daily tasks. But foster parents can also do so much more for you as your mentor. They can help you develop and meet your goals. They can show you a way of life you never even imagined. They can show you how to become independent, respectable, and resourceful. Make sure someone is fulfilling this key role in your life. Take it from me, not everything has to be learned the hard way.

Be cautious as to who you elect to be a mentor. This should be a person who makes good decisions and supports your goals. This person should be caring, professional, and honorable. You have to use common sense when you are selecting a mentor. If the person is negative and disrespectful, clearly he or she will not make a good mentor. People who discourage you from meeting your goals are not fit for this role. A good rule of thumb is a mentor should have similar characteristics to the list you developed in Chapter One. A great mentor will have your best interests in mind.

Summary of Actions:
1. Find someone who has either been where you are or someone of influence (such as a foster parent, teacher, or a coach).
2. Make a list of questions to ask about learning life skills and obtaining your goals.

3. Listen to the response. If you receive a positive feeling about his or her response, then follow that advice. If you receive a negative feeling about his or her response, then be gracious and politely exit the conversation.
4. Find mentor's for different areas in life. For example, if your goal is to go to college, find a teacher or guidance counselor who can help you explore and prepare.
5. Keep a written list of your mentors. Don't forget to add to that list often.
6. Continuously thank your mentors for their time, energy, and guidance.

Take Away:

Having a mentor helps identify a more focused path and creates a well-rounded individual by encouraging you to keep improving and breaking you from your comfort zone.

Chapter Four: Beat the Stigma

Foster Care Wisdom:
"New beginnings are often disguised as painful endings." – Lao Tzu

Mile Marker:
If you go through life being told that you are going to fail, more than likely you will start to believe this. As a foster child, you may feel that people expect you to fail. The participants in the study felt similarly. Why wouldn't they? Again, just reference the statistics identified earlier. As a foster child, you may feel the burden of the negative stigma associated with foster care. However, foster children everywhere have the power to change this misunderstanding. Do not keep failing. Do not continue the cycle. Break the mold. Shatter the stereotypes. Sadly, some teachers, guidance counselors, and other school personnel expect little more than the status quo from foster children. The Vera Institute of Justice found that even foster parents, some of whom have little formal education themselves, and caseworkers, who are meant to advocate for their charges, may expect nothing more than a passing grade from a foster child. They also found that few foster children are encouraged to think about college and are not encouraged to participate in the extra-curricular activities associated with higher academic achievement. Expect more from yourself and be better.

Furthermore, foster children must utilize this stigma positively. You may be familiar with the expression, "She has a chip on her shoulder," which means, simply, an individual is upset or holding a grudge against something or someone. As stated in Chapter One, remain positive and do not focus on the negatives. If you identify with the expression, use it for motivation. If you are upset at your family or your past life, use that energy as impetus to rise above. Don't think about the past; rather, remember you are a foster child overcoming life's toughest challenges. Use the "chip on your shoulder" attitude as fuel for your fire. Use this to motivate you to want to prove yourself or others wrong and succeed in life.

Moreover, this idea does not have to be complex or lengthy. Use how others may feel about you as momentum to succeed. Do not succumb to their pity or low expectations. Instead, show them that you are capable of so much more. Your ability to succeed is not limited to the address in which you currently reside or the composition of your family. You do not have to replicate what others have done before you. You can use this doubt as a force in your life to excel. Make this "chip" translate into tangible, positive actions.

Discussion:
"I don't strive for the center of attention. I strive to prove people wrong. It's kind of like they don't get interested in your life until you do something good. I want them to know that this didn't break me, and I'm stronger than what a lot of what my relatives were. I think it's kind of like a chip on my shoulder. I do want to show people this isn't something that's going to break me." Research Participant/Former Foster Child

I remember being a young kid in foster care and having to explain the awkwardness of my situation. When other kids asked what my parents do or why we moved to their town, all I could do was lie, but I knew sooner or later that people would find out the truth. I was ashamed of being a foster child. I was ashamed of my family for allowing this to happen. I was ashamed of myself for allowing this to happen, which is completely absurd. This is not your fault, and there is no reason to feel ashamed, but we all do. After a few months of being in foster care, I started to identify with this negative stigma.

"I don't strive for the center of attention. I strive to prove people wrong. It's kind of like they don't get interested in your life until you do something good. I want them to know that this didn't break me, and I'm stronger than what a lot of what my relatives were. I think it's kind of like a chip on my shoulder. I do want to show people this isn't something that's going to break me."

Research Participant/Former Foster Child

I didn't know exactly what it was at the time, only that it was a weird feeling. I knew people genuinely cared about me and wanted to help me, but it's still a weird feeling. I was friends with the kids in my school but I always felt as though I was a second-rate friend. I felt as though I was a friend who they were ashamed of. I started to get extremely angry. This anger hurt me in school and got me into a lot of trouble. I was upset at life and wanted people to know it.

I used the negative stigma as a crutch that only ignited the belief I would become a failure. I didn't realize the opportunity I had at that moment. I could have used that anger as motivation to prove people wrong. I could have used the anger to do better in school, focus harder on sports, and become a better person. But, like so many other foster children, I fell in line with the stigma for a while. It took a long time to realize how good it would feel to do well and prove people wrong. I remember small achievements and the feelings I had from them. I distinctly remember becoming the starting running back on my high school football team. That felt good!

"I refuse to be a delinquent. I don't want to be a statistic. I don't' want to be a delinquent; I don't want to live and survive off other people. And that's what I think a lot of people are doing. Living off the government, having so many kids, not being able to afford to take care of their kids.

> *"I refuse to be a delinquent. I don't want to be a statistic. I don't' want to be a delinquent; I don't want to live and survive off other people. And that's what I think a lot of people are doing. Living off the government, having so many kids, not being able to afford to take care of their kids. I can't be like that. I got to do something with my life. I'm an eager person. I'm eager to graduate; I'm eager to educate myself. Education is the most important thing to me. Being the fact that I was deprived of it as a child, it's more important to me now. And just graduating from college, it's so important to me."*
>
> Research Participant/Former Foster Child

31

"I can't be like that. I got to do something with my life. I'm an eager person. I'm eager to graduate; I'm eager to educate myself. Education is the most important thing to me. Being the fact that I was deprived of it as a child, it's more important to me now. And just graduating from college, it's so important to me." Research Participant/Former Foster Child

Channeling your anger into motivation is going to be a key to your success. I feel confident many of you feel the twinge in your gut, angry at your situation. Use that anger! As Frank Sinatra once said, "the best revenge is massive success." Use your aggressions, fears, and disappointments to your advantage. Pay close attention to the steps in the summary of actions.

Summary of Actions:
1. Stop and think about what makes you angry.
2. Create a list of the negative thoughts in your head.
3. Review your list and turn all those negative thoughts into positive actions. If you are upset at the circumstance that landed you in foster care, alter that into an advantage.
4. Think about the positive outcomes that stem from changing negatives into a positive. For example, you may be a foster child, but you are now out of a neglectful home with the unique opportunity to create a better life. You have more advantages now than you had before.
5. Allow the situation to become motivation. People will expect you to fail. You came from nothing and can create something. Success is yours to take.

Take Away:
Use your anger and aggression in a positive way. Stop feeling sorry for yourself and stop feeling ashamed about being a foster child. You now have more benefits than the majority of the kids in your class.

Chapter Five: Understand Your Benefits

Foster Care Wisdom:
"Life takes on meaning when you become motivated, set goals and charge after them in an unstoppable manner." – Les Brown

Mile Marker:
As a foster child, there are many benefits available for your consumption. It is imperative that you are aware of these benefits and take full advantage of them. When developing your exit plan as you age out of the system, ensure that you know what benefits are available and how to utilize them.

Federal law requires that you are provided a personalized transition plan during the ninety day period before you turn eighteen or are scheduled to leave foster care. As a foster child, you may be eligible for specific benefits and training. Ask for them! The following list identifies potential assistance you are eligible to receive in addition to education benefits to attend college. Make sure to speak with your caseworker or independent living coordinator about these benefits.

Life Skills Training:

1. Health and safety
2. Housing and transportation
3. Job readiness
4. Financial management
5. Life decisions and responsibility
6. Personal and social relationships

Supportive Services:

1. Graduation items
2. Counseling
3. Tutoring
4. Driver's education fees
5. Mentoring

You may also receive a monthly transitional living allowance once you exit the foster care system. Depending on the availability of funds, you can receive aftercare room and board assistance. This assistance will help you pay for rent, utilities, security deposits, and food. You will need to contact your independent living coordinator and caseworker to discuss these benefits.

The benefits identified are important to research. Not only are you potentially eligible for monetary benefits, but you may also receive life skills development. As mentioned before, you must be ready to be a self-sufficient adult when you exit foster care. Some of the available services will assist you with this goal. As you gain confidence in your life skills, you will start to gain more self-esteem. As you gain more self-esteem, you will start to develop new skills and this will open up new opportunities. Take advantage of the services that are provided to you. Use these services to develop your life building skills and skills necessary to develop relationships.

Furthermore, as you prepare for adulthood, you must gradually increase your responsibilities and gain more control of your life. You should have a caseworker that you communicate with regularly as a foster child. That caseworker may not necessarily be your mentor, but it is still your responsibility to ask questions about the resources available to you. Take charge of your future by proactively asking your caseworker about your entitlements.

Additionally, foster parents can also find different types of assistance. The U.S. government website, www.benefits.gov, informs citizens of benefits they may be eligible for and provides information on how to apply for assistance. Some of the benefits foster parents may be eligible for are the following:

1. Child care resource and referral service
2. Child tax credit
3. Child and dependent care credit
4. Family planning services
5. Head start and early head start
6. Grants
7. Special improvement projects
8. Special education

As a foster child, several services and resources exist to ensure you receive the support you need to be an independent adult. You may have to be your own advocate to receive these benefits, but do not let them go unused. This is another reason to embrace your placement in foster care. Without this system, you may not be exposed to these services in your own biological home and may have little to no support when you become an adult. Take advantage of all of the resources at your disposal.

Discussion:

"I'm still trying to figure it out. I'm not sure how it works." Research Participant/Former Foster Child

"I don't remember when I first met with my independent living coordinator with SRS. I think it was at the end of my last semester. I had already been accepted into college." Research Participant/Former Foster Child

It was painfully obvious that the foster care system let quite a few children down by not properly explaining benefits, specifically education benefits to these kids. The participants in the study felt that foster children did not use their benefits because they were informed too late.

Some participants indicated they were not notified of their benefits until they were eighteen years old. That is way too late! Just like planning for any other goal you have set, you will need to plan ahead to receive these benefits by the time you actually need to use them.

"I'm still trying to figure it out. I'm not sure how it works."

Research Participant/Former Foster Child

"I don't remember when I first met with my independent living coordinator with SRS. I think it was at the end of my last semester. I had already been accepted into college."

Research Participant/Former Foster Child

Participants had to figure out a lot on their own, but it doesn't have to be that way. Start communicating with your caseworker and foster parents early on about your plans when you exit foster care. Inform them you need to start meeting with someone to develop this plan. I cannot emphasize enough how important it is to utilize the people and resources available to you during your placement in foster care. There are many outstanding benefits waiting to be used in your pursuit of becoming a successful adult. Advocate for yourself and ask questions about your eligibility. Make sure you get as much material as you can from your caseworker and take diligent notes.

If you are close to high school graduation, contact your caseworker immediately and go over your exit plan. If you are not close to exiting, contact him or her for planning purposes. If you complete the steps in the Summary of Actions you will be leaps and bounds ahead of your peers. The following questions are sure to leave your caseworker speechless.

Summary of Actions:
1. Get the name and contact information for your caseworker.
2. Contact your caseworker once a week to go over your benefits.
3. Create a list of questions to ask your caseworker. These questions will depend on your age and academic year in school.
4. At a minimum, you will want to ask the following questions:
   - Am I eligible for cash benefits?
   - Am I eligible for healthcare and dental assistance?
   - Am I eligible for tuition assistance for college?
   - Can you assist me in getting in contact with a specific college?
   - Can you assist me with an application for a specific college?
   - What organizations can I join in order to become more socially active?

- Will I be appointed a Court Appointed Special Advocate (CASA)? The answer should be yes. Find out who it is and stay in contact with this person. Use them as a mentor. (I still use mine today. She is one of the greatest ladies I have ever met!)
- What additional benefits am I eligible for?

Take Away:

Ask questions and find out about your benefits. Do not wait for someone to provide you with this information because that may not happen.

Chapter Six: Use Your Education Benefits

Foster Care Wisdom:
"Education is the most powerful weapon which you can use to change the world." – Nelson Mandela

Mile Marker:
Education can be linked to success in just about every scenario you consider. In foster care, this might just be the "key" to success. The problem is that most foster children grow up in families where education is not emphasized. This population is inexperienced in the application, enrollment, and financial aid processes associated with attending college. Foster children struggle without a mentor to illustrate the road map to plod through this process.

If you remember the statistics from research discussed earlier, only 2% of foster children graduate from college. Just think about that—only 2%! This is an embarrassingly low amount of success rates among foster children. As a foster child, you have a golden ticket to go to college. It's imperative that you understand your benefits and how to use them because without these benefits, life will once again become difficult. Education benefits allotted for foster care children is the only reason the research participants were able to attend college.

Moreover, the foster care system will assist you in paying for college. Just make sure you pay attention to the specific age requirements and be mindful of the expiration of your benefits. The foster care system has set up an Education and Training Voucher (ETV) program. This is a federally funded and state-administered program. You may be eligible to receive up to $5,000 in financial assistance per year to help reach your goals. This is in addition to federal grants and scholarships you may also be eligible for. The ETV requirements are as follows:

Meet college enrollment requirements and be enrolled in at least six semester hours in an accredited school. Students must attend a public or non-profit program that provides a bachelor's degree or not less than a two-year program providing credit towards a degree or certification; or a one-year program of training to prepare students for employment.

Students participating in the ETV program on their 21st birthday may remain eligible until the month of their 23rd birthday so long as they are enrolled in ETV and making satisfactory academic progress. However, speak with your caseworker or independent living coordinator regarding this policy.

Youth in foster care are eligible for ETV if they are at least sixteen and likely to remain in care until eighteen; or

Youth who aged out of foster care, but have not yet turned twenty-one; or

Youth who were adopted after turning age sixteen and are not yet twenty-one; or

Youth who enter permanency care assistance after age sixteen.

You may also be eligible for specific expenses paid by ETV. Some of these expenses include books, computers, child care, and transportation. Specific states will also provide college tuition fee waivers if you attend college at state supported institutions. Depending on funding availability, you may be eligible for vocational or certification courses, housing assistance, and additional healthcare benefits. It is highly probable with planning and careful financial management that you can complete an undergraduate degree completely debt free.

Additionally, researchers from CNN conducted a study in 2013 that found the average student loan debt to be $29,400. In fact, seven in ten seniors graduate with student loan debt. They also found that student loan debt has risen at an average rate of 6% per year from 2008 to 2012. In 2013, the Huffington Post found that the average debt of $29,400 is actually up 63% in less than a decade. You have an edge over nearly everyone else. You have an opportunity to have your school paid for. You need to use these benefits while they are there to be used.

Education provides you the knowledge, confidence, and skills to further yourself in life. The foster care system provides you the resources to attain this education. And, most importantly, you provide the motivation and determination to achieve excellence.

Discussion:

"My father and mother, they didn't have a proper education. My mother dropped out of school when she was sixteen." Research Participant/Former Foster Child

Education is something that no one can take away from you. Education is a common way to identify success and a traditional way to earn a decent income. More doors will open for you as you attain more education. I remember the job opportunities that opened for me once I received my bachelor's degree. I went from applying for jobs that made $8.00 an hour to applying for jobs that made $50,000 annually. After I completed my master's degree, I started applying for jobs that made over $70,000 annually.

Success is not just about making a lot of money, but I know what is going through the mind of a foster child. You came from a poor family and you want a better life. One way to a better life is obtaining financial freedom. There is nothing wrong with wanting to make money; however, do not let this goal turn into your only driving force. Become aware of the opportunities that a college degree will provide you.

"Personally, I think education is success. I honestly think education is key to a better future. Because what else are you going to do? Work at McDonald's for the rest of your life because you don't have a degree? You can't make ends meet with that." Research Participant/Former Foster Child

"My father and mother, they didn't have a proper education. My mother dropped out of school when she was sixteen."

Research Participant/Former Foster Child

"Personally, I think education is success. I honestly think education is key to a better future. Because what else are you going to do? Work at McDonald's for the rest of your life because you don't have a degree? You can't make ends meet with that."

Research Participant/Former Foster Child

You will understand the importance of education once you start thinking about your goals in life. Some goals are unattainable without a college degree. If you want to become a doctor, you will need to be in school for quite some time. You will need to make your way to medical school. If you want to become an engineer, you will need to go through four to five grueling years of college to attain your specific degree. If you want to become a teacher, you will need to complete a specific degree plan and obtain certification. If you want to become a lawyer, you will need to attend college then make your way to law school. If you think about it, no matter what your goal is you will most likely have to go to college.

"Knowing that I'll be graduating after four years in college with no debt, unlike some kids who are twenty or thirty thousand dollars in debt. They ask me how I pay for my degree, and I say the State of Kansas pays for me. If you were moved of out your parents' house at a young age and you had no one to go to and then you've been offered by the state to go to college and you go to college for free, like who wouldn't take that? If you're a foster kid and the state is paying for you to go to college and you don't take it up, then you're stupid." Research Participant/Former Foster Child

> *"Knowing that I'll be graduating after four years in college with no debt, unlike some kids who are twenty or thirty thousand dollars in debt. They ask me how I pay for my degree, and I say the State of Kansas pays for me. If you were moved of out your parents' house at a young age and you had no one to go to and then you've been offered by the state to go to college and you go to college for free, like who wouldn't take that? If you're a foster kid and the state is paying for you to go to college and you don't take it up, then you're stupid."*
>
> Research Participant/Former Foster Child

There are so many benefits that you are eligible for just by simply being a foster child. This is why being a foster child is an opportunity. My hope is that you understand the importance of an education. While college may seem like a daunting expedition, there are many resources available to assist you. Follow these steps to make life simpler:

Summary of Actions:
1. Contact your caseworker and set up a meeting to discuss your exit plan and your education benefits. If you are preparing to exit the foster care system, you may want to schedule this interview with your independent living coordinator.
2. Have your caseworker review and provide you a list of your education benefits. Have them identify the steps you must take in order to obtain your ETV when you become the appropriate age.
3. Find out if there is a specific tuition fee waiver for a state school.
4. Meet with your guidance counselor to identify prospective schools and majors.
5. Identify at least three schools you are interested in. Again, if you do not have a preference, find a state supported institution/school. If you already know your major or what you want to study, use this to identify your schools of choice.
6. Bring your list to your caseworker and go over the application process if you have reached the appropriate age. Contact the schools you are interested in and apply early so you do not miss any deadlines.
7. Determine any important deadline dates. Keep track of these dates so you do not miss registration, admittance programs, or financial aid snafus, and leave plenty of time to meet requirements.
8. Schedule the SAT or ACT. Most colleges will take one or the other; however, contact your school to see if they require one or both of them.

9. Speak with your foster parents and caseworker. Set up visits with your top schools during your junior and senior year of high school.

10. Contact the school's business, registrar, and financial aid office. Start working with those offices early so you can accurately identify how to ensure everything is paid. You will have to complete a Free Application for Federal Student Aid (FASFA). Information can be found at https://fafsa.ed.gov.

11. Don't forget to apply for scholarships! Use your challenges and triumphs to make your application stand out.

12. Speak with your guidance counselor about completing college credits while you are still in high school. This is a great way to get a head of the game.

13. Focus on your grades. The better your grades and test scores, the better the chance you have of getting accepted into the college of your choice. Your grades and test scores do matter.

14. You may need to obtain letters of recommendation. This is where you can use your mentor list from Chapter Three. Ask your mentors for them to write a letter on your behalf, and make sure you thank them. Hand written thank you letters are a common courtesy. Be gracious of those attempting to help, no matter how stressful or overwhelming the process can be.

Take Away:
Start thinking about your future now. Dictate what your purpose in life will be.

Chapter Seven: Become Socially Active

Foster Care Wisdom:

"I alone cannot change the world, but I can cast a stone across the waters to create many ripples." – Mother Teresa

Mile Marker:

Negative stigma associated with being a foster child may prevent you from wanting to be around other people. Most of us at one time or another are ashamed that we were foster children. This is a normal feeling and it's easy to see why so many foster children have social issues during their lives. However, it is crucial that you become socially active and develop valued interpersonal skills. Gain socially active exposure to different people, ideas, and opinions. It is important that you form relationships from all walks of life. This is the best way to learn what kind of life you want to lead.

Moreover, becoming socially active may be scary or risky. It will require that you share part of your life with others. Again, this is where you can share your positivity about the opportunities foster care provides. Facing and overcoming fear is a developmental milestone that everyone encounters. You will be a stronger, more confident individual when you no longer let fear stand in your way. This is where the power of positive thinking is important. If you want to be successful, you must understand how to interact with other people. This is more difficult as you age out of foster care.

Developing skills to be socially active comes with practice. Just as in developing any ability or skill, you must practice in order to develop these skills. Practice this skill by engaging in conversations with new people, by joining different organizations that share your positive goals, and by building connections with people who support you. If you feel as though you lack social skills, you must practice even harder. Practice interacting with a variety of people and take risks in letting your guard down. Find people you believe to be skilled with social interaction and model your behaviors after them.

Research participants repeatedly indicated the importance of being socially active and seeking out leadership opportunities. Their involvement in the social realm was pivotal in their success upon exiting the foster care system. This is a best practice identified by former foster care children and should be top priority on your list of goals.

Discussion:
"I think communication with mentors and organizations is key. I can interact with kids that are in my situation and members are like all successful, doing good in school."
Research Participant/Former Foster Child

There is definitely a sense that being socially active is instrumental in the success of a foster child. The participants in the study participated in many different youth advisory councils. These programs empowered the participants to provide advice and guidance regarding child welfare. This is where they found their voices. One participant became the Vice President of the Kansas Youth Advisory Council (KYAC), a huge achievement.

"During my sophomore year of high school when my case manager brought me to KYAC, I was able to relate to other kids in similar circumstances. And with that, they helped me to feel more accepted...I was not only talking to other people who had experienced what I had experienced, but as a whole we were more glued together."
Research Participant/Former Foster Child

"I think communication with mentors and organizations is key. I can interact with kids that are in my situation and members are like all successful, doing good in school."

Research Participant/Former Foster Child

"During my sophomore year of high school when my case manager brought me to KYAC, I was able to relate to other kids in similar circumstances. And with that, they helped me to feel more accepted...I was not only talking to other people who had experienced what I had experienced, but as a whole we were more glued together."

Research Participant/Former Foster Child

Furthermore, participants in my study highly recommended participating in these councils. These organizations helped with the development of strengths and skill sets. The organizations also provided them with a unique outlet to achieve their goals and speak their minds to people with similar experiences.

"I have been nominated by the leaders of KYAC to represent the state of Kansas at Washington D.C., at a youth convention center for the National Youth Transition Database. For me, that was definitely an honor because I never thought they would pick me for something like that. To represent them is just amazing to me, and being able to give my opinion over things is just amazing." Research Participant/Former Foster Child

Take advantage of all the different organizations you can participate in. As I discussed before, get involved with different youth advisory councils and leadership initiatives. Participate in different athletic and academic teams. Participating on teams will assist you in developing leadership skills and forming close relationships with your peers. Being part of a team forces you to be socially interactive and pushes you to be involved for a greater purpose.

I highly suggest participating in religious and spiritual organizations if you are a spiritual person. This is another avenue to become socially active and feel good at the same time. The power of prayer can be a very important tool for those who believe in a higher power.

> *"I have been nominated by the leaders of KYAC to represent the state of Kansas at Washington D.C., at a youth convention center for the National Youth Transition Database. For me, that was definitely an honor because I never thought they would pick me for something like that. To represent them is just amazing to me, and being able to give my opinion over things is just amazing."*
>
> Research Participant/Former Foster Child

Summary of Actions:
1. Ask your foster parents, caseworker, independent coordinator, or teacher's what type of organizations to participate in. These may be foster care-specific organizations or other teams/organizations.
2. Create a list of groups that interest you, and sign up for them.
3. Participate in a youth advisory council. Participating in these organizations will provide you with a voice on policy development and decision-making related to the needs of youth in your community.
4. Participate in as many athletic organizations as possible.
5. Participate in as many academic teams as possible. Become an active participant in your school's speech and/or debate program.
6. Develop presentation skills and get used to speaking in front of people.
7. If you are a religious person, find a religious organization aligned with your beliefs and participate regularly. Identify the importance of prayer and develop a close relationship with God.

Take Away:
Be brave and bold. Become socially active to develop crucial communication, leadership, and interpersonal skills. You have an interesting perspective that organizations need to hear. Joining organizations will allow you the opportunity to learn from others as well.

Chapter Eight: After Foster Care

Foster Care Wisdom:
"If opportunity doesn't knock, build a door." – Milton Berle

Mile Marker:
There are many opportunities available to you as you exit the foster care system. It is an exciting time to have the freedom and independence to pursue your goals. The foster care system should have assisted you in becoming a self-sufficient adult and in building the path towards a successful life. Take advantage of the many great opportunities offered to you during this phase of life.

As discussed in previous chapters, attaining a college degree provides you with a great number of opportunities. Do not just think of a four-year university when discussing college. Two–year or vocational schools also offer a great education and vast potential. Degrees from a two-year or vocational school will allow you to enter directly into a wide array of fields such as medical, automotive, heating and air, air traffic control, and much more. Admission requirements may also be different if you apply to a two-year or vocational school. Cost for tuition is usually lower at two-year schools. These schools serve as a good option if you do not meet four-year university admission requirements. This avenue is a great option if you simply want to complete general education courses with the intent of transferring to a four-year school. If you choose the college route, learn about your additional benefits beyond the tuition fee waiver and ETV program.

Moreover, if you are considering joining the military, you have plenty of options.

Reserve Officer Training Corps (ROTC) offers several scholarships to students accepted into this program. This could be a great way to receive a full-tuition scholarship. After successful completion of ROTC you will be a commissioned officer in your service branch.

Enlist in the military. By enlisting in the military, you may be eligible for bonuses up to $20,000. You will also be eligible for the Montgomery G.I. Bill and tuition assistance. If you join the military, think outside the box and identify a career path that will lead to a civilian job. You can obtain jobs in the military in just about any career field you can think of. You can obtain jobs in a variety of fields, including administrative support, military intelligence, legal support, law enforcement, mechanics, computers, medical, construction, engineering, transportation, or aviation.

Obtain a medical degree through the military. The military is in need of doctors, nurses, therapists, and other medical professionals. In some situations, they will send you to training and pay you to complete a degree. Can you think of any other employer who will do this?

Most colleges will accept military training as college credit. Depending on the training, you can knock out several college credits just by completing training.

Joining the military will not only provide you with outstanding benefits, but this branch of the government will teach you superb leadership skills.

Additionally, there are other avenues to explore in order to find success after foster care. You can even obtain money for college while helping people at the same time. College may not be the right choice for you or you may need some additional time to get ready for school. Education is a lifelong journey and you can take an incremental approach to an education or a career. Service organizations may provide you with the path you feel is most successful:

AmeriCorps: This organization is an education and work experience opportunity in one. You will learn teamwork, leadership skills, and life building skills. Most AmeriCorps members receive student loan deferment and training, and may receive a living allowance and health insurance. For more information visit www.nationalservice.gov.

Teach for America: This outfit looks for individuals who show leadership potential and have other traits found in their most successful teachers. They offer competitive salaries as well as health insurance, retirement benefits, and may include federal loan forbearance. For more information visit www.teachforamerica.org.

The Peace Corps: This opportunity sends Americans abroad to assist with the needs of the world. They offer a stipend for living costs, reimbursement for travel, an AmeriCorps education grant, student loan forgiveness, and eligibility for college credit for service. For more information visit http://www.peacecorps.gov.

Job Corps: This is a free education and training program that helps young people learn a career, earn a high school diploma or GED, and obtain employment. For more information visit http://www.jobcorps.gov.

Leaving foster care is the close of one chapter and open of another. This is an exciting, but often scary adventure. Stay focused or your life may spiral in a direction you never intended. Beyond foster care, stay in contact with those you have identified as mentors. Stay positive while eliminating doubt. This will be a very trying time in your life, but if you remain positive, you will succeed.

To be successful in today's world, you need to be comfortable with the uncomfortable. Really think about that phrase. You have already found mechanisms of dealing with the uncomfortable. Leave your comfort zone and take life by the horns. If opportunity comes your way, then take it, especially if that means entering the unknown. The earlier you are comfortable with the uncomfortable and unknown the better off your chances at being successful. If that means accepting a job in another state or getting accepted into a school hundreds of miles away, jump at the chance. Many people are afraid to leave their comfortable lives and take a chance. It is very frightening and uncomfortable taking risks. However, you have to take these opportunities when they present themselves. You have to leave your comfort zone to maximize your potential. You will never fully develop as a person until you identify the importance of becoming comfortable with the uncomfortable. "You miss 100% of the shots you don't take." – Wayne Gretzky.

Moreover, you must also give back in some way or another once you exit foster care. As a former foster child, who has found success, I feel obligated to give back and help others do the same. To give back does not necessarily mean you have to donate money. Giving back means helping others by sharing advice and experiences. My way of giving back is to continue to write about, speak to, and research foster care improvements.

51

As a former foster child who has obtained success, I feel obligated and want to share my positive experiences and research to assist you in obtaining success. The more you give back, the more you will actually receive. That's crazy to think about, right? It's true though—the more you give, the more opportunities will open up for you to give and receive.

You have opportunities to give back right now. Participate in youth advisory councils as mentioned in Chapter Seven. This is a way to tell your story and give advice to those with similar paths. Find ways to mentor younger foster children; help them through their experiences and celebrate their accomplishment. Shower them with positive motivation as your mentor has for you. Take this wisdom and assist another foster child. Supporting those new to the system by sharing your experiences can provide positive motivation for them, but it will also remind you to remain positive when thinking about your future.

When you give back, you show others that you truly care. As I stated before, you do not have to provide money to give back. Time and energy are often a greater and more meaningful contribution than money. Find a purpose and find a way to share that purpose with others. Participate in research associated with foster care and share your story. Find ways to make the foster care program better. Speak with your caseworker, foster parent, priest, teacher, or coach, and try to find ways to give back.

Moreover, this chapter should impact those of you who are out of foster care. Even if you are still searching for success and are having difficulties in life, you can still give back. You have stories and experiences to share with those who are currently in foster care. Find ways to speak to these kids and mentor them. If you have past failures, such as serving jail time or finding yourself homeless, share those experiences as a warning to others. You can give advice on how to avoid these and similar situations. We all have something to share that may help others.

Similarly, if you have found success, share your experiences as inspiration for others. Find ways to speak to foster children, foster parents, state agencies, and different people who can help the current system. Write a book! Start finding ways to present your story and do not lose motivation to share. We all have immense value as former foster children. We should all feel obligated to help out the next generation to break the stigma we were once subjected to.

Summary of Actions:
If you haven't already, clearly identify your desires in life. How do you imagine your future? What will you do to attain those goals?

1. Review your list of goals daily to stay motivated. Identifying these goals will greatly assist you in your next chapter of life.
2. If you did not earn a high school diploma, complete your General Educational Development (GED), which is equivalent to a high school diploma. The bottom line is that you must have a high school diploma or a GED to find any success in the future.
3. Research how to attain your goals. Use your mentors and available resources to determine how to best reach your goals.
4. Look into other alternatives that will assist you with money for school. Review this chapter and look into the excellent nonprofit organizations such as AmeriCorps.
5. If college isn't for you or you need more time to figure out what you want to do, start researching different job opportunities (but do not let your education benefits expire). Seek advice from your mentors, as they have your best interest in mind and are willing to go beyond to assist you in achieving your goals.
6. Compose a resume and update it regularly with each additional duty or job you master.

7. Network with anyone and everyone. You have already started networking by seeking mentors and interacting with them. Pay attention to the people you meet and pay attention to how you treat them and interact with them. You may meet a person who will assist you in getting into a school or obtaining a new job one day. The more people you meet and interact with, the more opportunities will come your way.

8. Participate in different networking events. Attend job fairs hosted by your community or college. Join organizations in college and fine tune your social networking skills.

9. Create a profile on LinkedIn and other sites that will help you with your future career. Remember to keep your online image clean, as this is a direct representation of your character. Prospective employers may search your name and find information you otherwise would not have wished to share. Think twice about what you post; if it doesn't help you, then don't post it.

10. Go after what you want. Don't let anyone get in your way. Remember to surround yourself by positive people and positive environments.

Take Away:

Get comfortable with the uncomfortable and be proud of all you have accomplished.

Chapter Nine: Final Thoughts

As I wrote this book, I thought many times, "Why didn't someone tell me this before? It would have been great to have this information when I was in foster care!" There are several paths to take to move towards success, but this one worked for me. This same route worked for participants in my study who had similar experiences to my own. The foster care system brings with it a negative stigma; however, there are so many opportunities available to you as a result of being a foster child. My study identified success stories from former foster children. I identified ten themes from my research and I used those themes as well as the concept of positive thinking to write this book. Every chapter, excluding the first, was built based on the foundation of these themes. Use these chapters as the foundation for your success. Each chapter holds an important step for attaining success in life. While you may disagree with some information in this book, focus on the points useful to you and make the steps reality.

Charles Kettering once said, "Believe and act as if it were impossible to fail." I live by this motto. I cannot fail; I will always triumph. This may sound difficult, but it truly is not. The biggest fight will take place in your mind. You will battle negative thoughts regularly, but remember that only you can decide who you will be tomorrow.

Additionally, with the help of this book, I hope you have recognized the importance of planning. The military has a saying: "Piss poor planning promotes piss poor performance." You have to plan properly or you will not get the results you desire. You have to plan and be prepared. Use the chapters of this book to help you prepare. Follow my roadmap and my summary of action for each chapter. I truly wish someone would have provided me with positive advice and motivation as a former foster child. Life would have been a lot easier!

If you have read through this book, you have the tools to be a success. Your success hinges on your commitment to the plan and to changing your future. Failure cannot be produced by another person; use the tools provided to design your own future. Think about how you can utilize the information from this book in your own personal experiences. The text explains specific actions you can take, but consider that there is still a lot of research for you to complete on your own. Being a foster child does not define you; rather, you define what it means to be a foster child. Change the stigma to positive by channeling positivity in all aspects of your daily existence. Life in foster care is a temporary solution, but success is permanent. Be the change you want to see.

Resources

Useful Websites for Foster Parents and Children:

Adopt US Kids
http://adoptuskids.org/for-families/state-adoption-and-foster-care-information

Click on your respective state once you make your way to this website. It will provide you with an abundance of useful information regarding foster and adoption licensing requirements, costs for fostering and adoption, agency contact and orientation information, parent support group contacts, and upcoming events.

Foster Care & Adoptive Community
http://www.fosterparents.com

This website will provide you great training for foster care and adoption relating to at-risk children.

National Foster Parent Association
http://nfpaonline.org

The National Foster Parent Association (NFPA) is a great organization to join or donate to. The organization advocates for foster children and their foster parents.

Foster Care to Success
http:///www.fc2success.org

Foster Care to Success (FC2S) is the oldest and largest national nonprofit organization working solely with college bound foster youth.

Casey Family Program
http://www.casey.org

Casey Family Program is the nation's largest operating foundation. They focus on foster care and improving the child welfare system.

Child Welfare League of America
http://www.cwla.org
Child Welfare League of America (CWLA) is the nation's largest and oldest child welfare organization.

Children's Bureau
http://www.acf.hhs.gov
Children's Bureau is a federal agency comprising of two bureaus within the Administration on Children, Youth and Families, Administration for Children and Families of the Department of Health and Human Services.

Children's Defense Fund
http://www.childrensdefense.org
Children's Defense Fund (CDF) promotes programs protecting children from poverty, abuse, and neglect.

Foster Care Alumni of America
http://www.fostercarealumni.org
Foster Care Alumni of America (FCAA) is a national non-profit association that is led by alumni of the foster care system.

National Court Appointed Special Advocates Association
http://www.casaforchildren.org
National Court Appointed Special Advocates (CASA) Association is a network of 955 programs that recruit, train, and support volunteers to represent the best interest of children.

National Foster Care Coalition
http://www.nationalfostercare.org
National Foster Care Coalition (NFCC) promotes the well-being of children, youth, and families impacted by the child welfare system.

National Resource Center for Permanency and Family Connections
http://www.nrcpfc.org
National Resource Center for Permanency and Family Connections (NRCPFC) is a training, technical assistance, and information services organization dedicated to help strengthen the capacity of child welfare.

College Information:

College Scorecard
http://www.whitehouse.gov/issues/education/higher-education/college-score-card
"College Scorecards" on the U.S. Department of Education's College Affordability and Transparency Center website is a great source to search for a college that fits your needs and desires.

You simply use the Scorecard to search and find information about your potential college, including affordability and value. You can search for a specific college or search by location, type of college, area of interest, degree and major, occupation, distance education, etc.

National Center for Education Statistics
https://nces.ed.gov/collegenavigator
College Navigator allows students to search for the school that is right for them. You can search through their database by entering the name of a school, intended degree program, preferred location of the school, degree level you are seeking, and the type of institution (community college or four-year university).

Financial Assistance for College
Free Application for Federal Student Aid
http://www.fafsa.ed.gov
This web application must be completed for each school year. Using your financial information, the government will determine your eligibility for grants, work-study, student loans, and state and institutional programs. This application is free to complete.

Fastweb Scholarship Search
http://www.fastweb.com
This website provides a database and information to apply for a variety of scholarships. After completing your profile, you can search scholarships for which you meet the eligibility requirements.

Salt
http://www.saltmoney.org
SALT™ is a free, nonprofit-backed resource that makes it simple for you to take control of your finances and student loans. It promotes responsible borrowing, financial literacy, and scholarships.

Healthcare Information
Medicaid
http://www.medicaid.gov
The federal Affordable Care Act (ACA) recognizes that young adults may have difficulty obtaining affordable, comprehensive health care coverage on their own and that the cost of coverage can interfere with plans for college or embarking on a career. As a result, the ACA permits young adults to remain on their parents' health insurance until the age of twenty-six. For youth who emancipate from foster care and do not have access to health insurance through their parents, the ACA provides continued coverage through Medicaid.

Health Insurance Marketplace
www.healthcare.gov
This is the official site of the Health Insurance Marketplace. See your health insurance choices.

Youth Law Center
http://www.ylc.org/
The Youth Law Center is a public interest law firm that works to protect children in the nation's foster care and justice systems from abuse and neglect. The YLC ensures that this population will receive the necessary support and services to become healthy and productive adults.

Additional Information:

GED Information:
If you did not complete high school, you MUST complete the General Educational Development (GED). Jurisdictions and states award a Certificate of High School Equivalency for individuals who receive a passing score on the GED. Visit http://www.gedtestingservice.com to schedule your test. There are guides available to help you prepare for the GED.

Career Planning and Resume Writing:

Occupational Outlook Handbook
http://www.bls.gov/ooh
Occupational Outlook Handbook provides job descriptions, job outlook and educational requirements for careers.

My Next Move
http://www.mynextmove.org
Browse careers by industry or take a career match test on this website.

Got Resume Builder
http://www.GotResumeBuilder.com
This resource guides people through the resume building process.

Best Sample Resume
http://www.bestsampleresume.com
Review sample resumes and cover letters to modify and perfect your own.

About the Author

Dr. Jamie Schwandt is a former foster child who understands how to succeed in life. He is currently a commissioned officer in the United States Army Reserve. Dr. Schwandt serves as a public speaker and has presented his research and personal story of challenges and triumphs for different foster care and social services organizations. He enjoys providing positive motivation for young individuals in foster care. He lives in Washington D.C. with his loving wife and family.

Dr. Schwandt had a difficult childhood and overcame significant obstacles to get where he is today. He was born in a small town in Kansas where his parents abused drugs and alcohol. Both parents battled depression while suffering from other mental health issues. His father committed suicide when he was eighteen years old. As a child, Dr. Schwandt witnessed many dangerous and poor decisions made by his parents. His mother suffered from severe drug addiction and alcoholism. He watched his mother use drugs in their home and was often left to take care of her and his younger brother.

He has vivid memories of seeing needles in the bathroom, witnessing domestic violence, and preventing his mother from multiple suicide attempts. Although Dr. Schwandt was able to overcome adversity, his younger brother did not adapt the same mentality and as a result continues to face challenges.

From birth to eighteen years old, Dr. Schwandt moved more than twenty times with his parents, grandparents, and in the foster care system. He enlisted in the United States Army Reserve when he was just seventeen years old and continues to serve his country as a commissioned officer. Despite the challenges he faced during his upbringing, Dr. Schwandt obtained a Bachelor of Science and Master of Science from Fort Hays State University. In May 2013, he completed a Doctor of Education (Ed.D.) from Kansas State University. Dr. Schwandt is both determined and tenacious and is blessed to have experienced many successes in life.

For inquiries about Dr. Schwandt speaking at your next event or conference contact **drjamieschwandt@gmail.com**.

<u>Starry Night Publishing</u>

Everyone has a story...

Don't spend your life trying to get published! Don't tolerate rejection! Don't do all the work and allow the publishing companies reap the rewards!

Millions of independent authors like you, are making money, publishing their stories now. Our technological know-how will take the headaches out of getting published. Let "Starry Night Publishing dot Com" take care of the hard parts, so you can focus on writing. You simply send us your Word document and we do the rest. It really is that simple!

The big companies want to publish only "celebrity authors," not the average book-writer. It's almost impossible for first-time authors to get published today. This has led many authors to go the self-publishing route. Until recently, this was considered "vanity-publishing." You spent large sums of your money, to get twenty copies of your book, to give to relatives at Christmas, just so you could see your name on the cover. Now, however, the self-publishing industry allows authors to get published in a timely fashion, retain the rights to your work, keeping up to seventy-percent of your royalties, instead of the traditional ten-percent.

We've opened up the gates, allowing you inside the world of publishing. While others charge you as much as ten-thousand dollars for a publishing package, we charge less than three-hundred dollars to cover proofreading, copyright, ISBN, and distribution costs. Do you really want to spend all your time formatting, converting, designing a cover, and then promoting your book, because no one else will?

Our editors are professionals, able to create a top-notch book that you will be proud of. Becoming a published author is supposed to be fun, not a hassle.

At Starry Night Publishing, you submit your work, we proofread it, create a professional-looking cover, a table of contents, compile your text and images into the appropriate format, convert your files for eReaders, take care of copyright information, assign an ISBN, allow you to keep one-hundred-percent of your rights, distribute your story worldwide on Amazon, Barnes & Noble and many other retailers, and write you a check for your royalties. There are no other hidden fees involved! You don't pay extra for a cover, or proofreading. You will never pay to keep your book in print. We promise! Everything is included! You even get a free copy of your book and unlimited discount copies.

In twelve short months, we've published more than three-hundred books, compared to the major publishing houses which only add an average of six new titles per year. We will publish your fiction, or non-fiction books about anything, and look forward to reading your stories and sharing them with the world.

We sincerely hope that you will join the growing Starry Night Publishing family, become a published author and gain the world-wide exposure that you deserve. You deserve to succeed. Success comes to those who make opportunities happen, not those who wait for opportunities to happen. You just have to try. Thanks for joining us on our journey.

www.starrynightpublishing.com

www.facebook.com/starrynightpublishing/

Made in the USA
Coppell, TX
22 February 2020